In the Spotlight

Lin-Manuel Miranda

by Kristine Spanier

Bullfrog
Books

Ideas for Parents and Teachers

Bullfrog Books let children practice reading informational text at the earliest reading levels. Repetition, familiar words, and photo labels support early readers.

Before Reading

- Discuss the cover photo. What does it tell them?

- Look at the picture glossary together. Read and discuss the words.

Read the Book

- "Walk" through the book and look at the photos. Let the child ask questions. Point out the photo labels.

- Read the book to the child, or have him or her read independently.

After Reading

- Prompt the child to think more. Ask: What did you know about Lin-Manuel Miranda before reading this book? What more would you like to learn about him after reading it?

Bullfrog Books are published by Jump!
5357 Penn Avenue South
Minneapolis, MN 55419
www.jumplibrary.com

Copyright © 2019 Jump! International copyright reserved in all countries. No part of this book may be reproduced in any form without written permission from the publisher.

Library of Congress Cataloging-in-Publication Data

Names: Spanier, Kristine, author.
Title: Lin-Manuel Miranda / by Kristine Spanier.
Description: Minneapolis, MN : Bullfrog Books, [2018]
Series: In the spotlight | Includes index.
Identifiers: LCCN 2018009697 (print)
LCCN 2018007985 (ebook)
ISBN 9781641280457 (ebook)
ISBN 9781641280433 (hardcover : alk. paper)
ISBN 9781641280440 (pbk.)
Subjects: LCSH: Miranda, Lin-Manuel, 1980
Juvenile literature. | Actors—United States
Biography—Juvenile literature.
Composers—United States—Biography
Juvenile literature. | Lyricists—United States
Biography—Juvenile literature.
Classification: LCC PN2287.M6446 (print)
LCC PN2287.M6446 S63 2019 (ebook)
DDC 792.02/8092 [B]—dc23
LC record available at https://lccn.loc.gov/2018009697

Editor: Jenna Trnka
Designer: Molly Ballanger

Photo Credits: Mindy Small/Getty, cover; Nicholas Hunt/Getty, 1, 20–21; Walter McBride/Getty, 3; Tinseltown/Shutterstock, 4; Theo Wargo/Getty, 5, 10–11, 13, 23tr; Brent N. Clarke/Getty, 6–7, 23mr; Jason Kempin/Getty, 8–9, 23tl; Kevin Mazur/Getty, 9, 23br; National Gallery of Art/Getty, 10; Kris Connor/Getty, 12, 23ml; HBO/Kobal/REX/Shutterstock, 14–15; Alberto E. Rodriquez/Getty, 16–17; Paul Morigi/Getty, 18, 23bl, 24; Gladys Vega/Getty, 19; Eloi _ Omelia/iStock, 22l; a katz/Shutterstock, 22m; Kathy SeaRick1/Shutterstock, 22r.

Printed in the United States of America at Corporate Graphics in North Mankato, Minnesota.

Table of Contents

Lin-Manuel

This is Lin-Manuel.

He is famous.

Why?

He writes musicals.

He is in them, too.

One is about his life.

The actors rap.

He wrote another one.

It is called *Hamilton*.

What is it about?

A man who helped
form our country.

Alexander
Hamilton

It won many awards.

award

Wow!

award

Lin is an actor.

He is in movies.

He is on TV shows.

He writes music
for movies, too.

Like what?

Moana!

Dwayne
Johnson

Lin started a charity.

Why? To help people.

Unity March
for Puerto Rico

18

He helps people
in Puerto Rico.

19

Lin loves to help others.

Key Events

January 16, 1980: Lin-Manuel Miranda is born in New York City, New York.

September 5, 2010: Miranda marries scientist and lawyer Vanessa Nadal.

April 18, 2016: *Hamilton* wins the Pulitzer Prize for drama.

March 9, 2008: *In the Heights,* Miranda's first musical, officially opens on Broadway. It wins four Tony Awards, including best musical.

August 6, 2015: *Hamilton* opens on Broadway.

May 3, 2016: *Hamilton* is nominated for 16 Tony Awards, the most in Broadway history.

Picture Glossary

actors
People who perform in a play, TV show, or movie.

famous
Very well-known to many people.

awards
Prizes given in honor of an achievement.

musicals
Plays or movies that include a lot of singing and dancing.

charity
An organization that raises money to help people in need or some other worthy cause.

rap
To speak words rhythmically to music.

Index

To Learn More

Learning more is as easy as 1, 2, 3.

1) Go to www.factsurfer.com

2) Enter "Lin-ManuelMiranda" into the search box.

3) Click the "Surf" button to see a list of websites.

With factsurfer.com, finding more information is just a click away.